W9-BEY-449

This is the First Holy Communion book of

_____

A gift from _____

I was baptized at _____

on _____

My godparents are

_____

_____

I first came to the table of the Lord

at _____ on _____

**Dedicated to the Catholic Community at Colorado College.
Sursum corda!**

Prayer texts on pages 55 through 64, except as noted, are reprinted from *Catholic Household Blessings and Prayers* © 1988 United States Catholic Conference, Inc., Washington DC. All rights reserved. Used with permission. The translation of the Magnificat on page 62 is by Anne Carter. Text © 1988 Society of the Sacred Heart. Excerpts from the English translation of the Order of Mass from *The Roman Missal* © 1973, International Committee on English in the Liturgy, Inc. (ICEL); excerpts from the English translation of *The Liturgy of the Hours* © 1974, ICEL; the English translation of the *Anima Christi* ("Soul of Christ") and the Prayer to the Guardian Angel from *A Book of Prayers* © 1982, ICEL. All rights reserved. English translation of *Gloria in Excelsis* and the Apostles' Creed by the International Consultation on English Texts.

MY FIRST HOLY COMMUNION © 2001 Liturgy Training Publications, 1800 North Hermitage Avenue, Chicago IL 60622-1101; 1-800-933-1800; fax 1-800-933-7094; orders@ltp.org. Website: www.ltp.org.

Editor, Gabe Huck; designer, M. Urgo; production editor, Audrey Novak Riley; production artist, Kari Nicholls.

LITURGY TRAINING PUBLICATIONS

Printed in China by Palace Press International.

Library of Congress Control Number: 2001087863

1-56854-252-6
HCOM

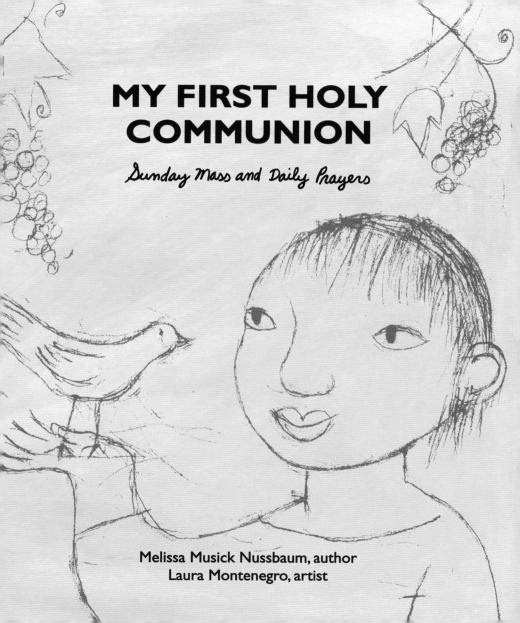

MY FIRST HOLY COMMUNION

Sunday Mass and Daily Prayers

Melissa Musick Nussbaum, author
Laura Montenegro, artist

To you who are now coming to the table of the Lord:

From the day of your baptism, the church prepared a place for you at the table of the Lord.

Every Sunday the baptized people gather around this table. And now you are called to come to that table, to taste and see the goodness of the Lord.

On the table are bread and wine. The good earth gives us wheat and gives us grapes.

Women and men harvest the wheat and grind it into flour and make bread. Men and women harvest the grapes and crush them and pour the juice into barrels, where it turns into wine.

So the table is set with gifts that earth has given and human hands have made. We pray that God will send the Holy Spirit upon these gifts so that the bread and wine become, for us, the body and blood of Christ.

Christ is our food. Christ is our drink.
All the hungry, thirsty church is called
to eat and drink at the table of the Lord.
We pray that God will send us out to
be the body of Christ for the world.

You come to this table with your
brothers and sisters. Sunday after
Sunday, for as long as you live, you
will raise your voice in song. You will
turn your ear to hear the story. You will
pray for those in need. You will offer
your hands in peace. You will walk in
procession to the table of the Lord.
You will do the loving work of Christ
in the world.

This book will help you find your way.
Learn by heart the words we say and
sing together.

Learn by heart the processions and the
gestures and the stillness that are part
of Sunday Mass.

Welcome to the table!

Have you ever seen a quilt?

Do you have a quilt?

Whether large or small, a quilt is made
of many tiny pieces of cloth.

Red pieces, blue pieces,
cotton pieces, silk pieces.

A quilt can be made of old baby clothes
or worn-out blue jeans
or brand new squares of fabric
fresh from the shop.

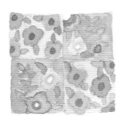

Think of all the work that goes into a quilt.

Someone gathers different kinds
and colors of cloth.

cloth scra

Someone cuts the cloth
into triangles or circles or squares.

Someone sews these many little pieces together
with stitches running up and stitches running down.

Then a border must be sewn
all around the edge,

and the quilt is done.

No one could stay warm under
a single scrap of cotton.

No one could wrap a child in
one small square of flannel.
But a whole quilt is thick and warm.

A quilt will protect you from the cold.

We can cuddle in a quilt
when we are lonely.

A quilt may bring us
sweet dreams.

A quilt will cover a bed
like a bright spill of flowers.

A quilt will lie on your
shoulders like a royal robe.

Every Sunday we gather for Mass.

Our journey to church begins at home.

Many people wake up early to wash and dress.
Others try for a little extra sleep.
Someone feeds the baby.
Someone helps us find socks that match
and gets all the shoelaces tied tight.

Perhaps we stop along the way to church
and bring neighbors or grandparents with us.

We are all like the pieces of a quilt
coming together.

This is our feast day.
We want to join hands,
to sing and to speak.

We come into church, all of us together.
We greet one another and begin to visit.

We ask about someone who is sick,
about a new baby, a trip,
the first day of school,
a missing tooth,
a job found, a job lost.

We look around and see the splashes of color and size
and shape spreading throughout the church.

In the name of the Father, and of the Son,
and of the Holy Spirit. Amen.

We begin to sing.
We keep time.
We keep rhythm.

Some of us walk
carrying the cross
and the candles
and our special book.

The song draws us
shoulder to shoulder,
hand to hand.

Our singing is like a thread
weaving up and down
and in and out,
stitching us together.

The Lord be with you.
And also with you.

We pray.

We give thanks to God for bringing us
from the east and the west,
from the north and the south,
from houses and apartments,
from shelters and the street
to this good place.

One God, forever and ever. Amen.

We sit quietly now because we want to hear our stories.
We want to hear how God spoke
and the world was created.
We want to hear how God called a people.

We want to hear surprising news, good news:
Even when the people forgot God,
God remembered them, always.

The book of readings is something
like a crazy quilt made up of
stories, poems, letters and visions.
This book is our treasure.

The word of the Lord. Thanks be to God.

We stand up and sing out our Alleluia.
We are getting ready to hear the gospel.

Glory to you, Lord.

We hear how Jesus came
to show us what God looks like.

God looks like a shepherd
leaving many sheep behind in order to search
the fields for one missing lamb.

God looks like a woman with ten silver coins.
When she loses one, she sweeps her whole house
searching for the coin.
And when she finds her lost treasure,
she calls all her friends to gather and rejoice.

Praise to you, Lord Jesus Christ.

We think of all the people, men and women, children and adults, all over the world.

God is stitching us, piece to piece, need to plenty, strength to weakness, sorrow to joy.

Now we stand again. We pray for the world.

We pray for the poor and for the church everywhere.

We pray for the sick. We pray for the dead.

We pray for those we will never meet,
whose names we will never know.

God knows each one by name.
So we can sing, "Lord, hear our prayer."

Lord, have mercy.
Christ, have mercy.
Lord, have mercy.

We bring everything before God.

We bring gifts of money.
We bring gifts of food.
We bring to the table the gifts
of bread and wine
we will bless and share.

This is God's table; it is our table.
We are welcome here.

Blessed be God forever.

Now the priest calls to us:
"Lift up your hearts!"

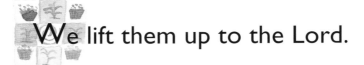 **W**e lift them up to the Lord.

We begin our praise to God
for all the wonders God has done and is doing
in our sight, in our hearing,
in our bread and wine,
in flesh and blood.

Holy, holy, holy Lord,
God of power and might,
heaven and earth are full of your glory.

"From age to age," we proclaim
with Christians throughout the world,
"you gather a people to yourself,
so that from east to west
a perfect offering may be made
to the glory of your name."

Hosanna in the highest.

We lift up our hearts and sing of Christ.
He is the Word through whom you made the universe,
the Savior you sent to redeem us.

By the power of the Holy Spirit
he took flesh and was born of the Virgin Mary.

For our sake he opened his arms on the cross;
he put an end to death and revealed his resurrection.

The priest prays to God:
"Let your Spirit come upon these gifts
to make them holy."

Then we remember what Jesus did
and how he loved us.

He took bread and gave you thanks.
He broke the bread, gave it to his disciples,
and said: "Take this, all of you, and eat it:
this is my body which will be given up for you."

When supper was ended, he took the cup.
Again he gave you thanks and praise,
gave the cup to his disciples, and said:
"Take this, all of you, and drink from it:
this is the cup of my blood."

Christ has died.
Christ is risen.
Christ will come again.

Lord, by your cross and resurrection
you have set us free.
You are the Savior
of the world.

We thank you for counting us worthy
to stand in your presence and serve you.
May all of us who share
in the body and blood of Christ
be brought together in unity
by the Holy Spirit.

Amen!

We cannot keep from singing:
Amen! Amen! Amen! Amen! Amen!
"Yes, and again, yes," we sing.

Always and forever.
"Yes," we sing, "may it be so."

We sing our Amen
until it spins out into the heavens,
like bright thread
joining all the Amens over all the earth.

Our Father, who art in heaven,
hallowed be thy name;
thy kingdom come;
thy will be done on earth
as it is in heaven.

Give us this day our daily bread;
and forgive us our trespasses
as we forgive those
who trespass against us;
and lead us not into temptation,
but deliver us from evil.

For the kingdom,
the power, and the glory
are yours, now and for ever.

Peace be with you.

Our union with God and with one another gives us strength. Alone, our edges would fray and unravel, but together, we are sturdy.

Lamb of God, have mercy on us.

The bread is being broken so all may share.
We are on the move now,
moving to the table God sets for us.

We are moving as one body, forward,
into the bounty of God.
We come with open hands, empty hands.
We come hungry and thirsty.

Lord, I am not worthy
to receive you,
but only say the word
and I shall be healed.

We come to be fed with bread and wine
that have become for us the body and blood
of our Lord Jesus Christ.

We come with our hands open
to receive the body and blood of Christ.

We take the bread and eat it.

We take the cup in our hands
and drink from it.

The body of Christ. Amen.
The blood of Christ. Amen.

We come singing together:

Taste and see,
  taste and see
     the goodness
        of the Lord.

When all have tasted the goodness of the Lord,
then we keep a quiet time.
We think of the wondrous life of God in us,
in this church that has shared the holy banquet.

Here we have received Christ.
We have remembered Christ's death and resurrection.
We have been filled with the gift of God
and the promise of glory to come.

Go in peace to love and serve the Lord.
Thanks be to God.

We have been blessed. We have been fed.
We are all sung out. We go out.
I will do my work. You will do your work.

We will pray.
We will visit the sick.
We will feed the hungry.

We will clothe the naked.
We will shelter the homeless.
We will teach. We will learn.

We will forgive.
We will ask forgiveness.
We will listen.
We will speak truth.
We will show mercy.
We will do peace.

teach and learn

pray

shelter the homeless

we will go out

visit the sick

clothe the naked

we will do our work

PRAYERS

For Sunday

When you tell about yourself, what do you say?
Do you say, "I am in the second grade at my school"?
Or do you say, "I have a little brother"? Or "I play
the piano"? A creed is a way we tell about ourselves
as the church. We are the people who hope in God.
This Creed says what we believe about God.

I believe in God, the Father almighty,
   creator of heaven and earth.

I believe in Jesus Christ, his only Son, our Lord.
   He was conceived by the power of the Holy Spirit
      and born of the Virgin Mary.
   He suffered under Pontius Pilate,
      was crucified, died, and was buried.
   He descended to the dead.
   On the third day he rose again.
   He ascended into heaven,
      and is seated at the right hand of the Father.
   He will come again to judge the living
      and the dead.

I believe in the Holy Spirit,
   the holy catholic Church,
   the communion of saints,
   the forgiveness of sins,
   the resurrection of the body,
   and the life everlasting. Amen.

We know who we are. We are the people God loves.
We are the people God forgives. We have the courage
to tell God everything, the wrong we have done and
the good we have failed to do. We call upon God's mercy
in this prayer:

**I confess to almighty God,
and to you, my brothers and sisters,
that I have sinned through my own fault
in my thoughts and in my words,
in what I have done,
and in what I have failed to do;
and I ask blessed Mary, ever virgin,
all the angels and saints,
and you, my brothers and sisters,
to pray for me to the Lord our God.**

After we receive holy communion, we can say this prayer:

**Soul of Christ, sanctify me.
Body of Christ, heal me.
Blood of Christ, drench me.
Water from the side of Christ, wash me.**

Every year at Christmas we hear the story of Jesus' birth. We hear how the angels cried out, "Glory to God in the highest." This hymn begins with those words:

Glory to God in the highest,
and peace to his people on earth.
Lord God, heavenly King,
almighty God and Father,
we worship you, we give you thanks,
we praise you for your glory.
Lord Jesus Christ, only Son of the Father,
Lord God, Lamb of God,
you take away the sin of the world:
have mercy on us.
You are seated at the right hand of the Father:
receive our prayer.
For you alone are the Holy One,
you alone are the Lord,
you alone are the Most High, Jesus Christ,
with the Holy Spirit,
in the glory of God the Father. Amen.

Morning Prayers

We begin each morning tracing the sign of who we are,
the sign of the cross. We make the sign: Now down, from
head to heart; now across, from shoulder to shoulder.

Once we were baptized in the name of the Father
and of the Son and of the Holy Spirit. We remember our
baptism every morning when we say:

**In the name of the Father, and of the Son,
and of the Holy Spirit. Amen.**

We thank God for every gift of the new day:

**Lord, open my lips,
and my mouth will proclaim your praise.**

**Glory to the Father, and to the Son,
and to the Holy Spirit:
as it was in the beginning,
is now, and will be for ever. Amen.**

While we are dressing, we say:

**Blessed are you, Lord, God of all creation:
you clothe the naked.**

When we are ready to go outside, we say:

**Blessed are you, Lord, God of all creation:
you guide my footsteps.**

Before we eat breakfast, we make the sign of the cross
and we say:

**Bless us, O Lord,
and these your gifts
which we are about to receive
from your goodness.
Through Christ our Lord.
Amen.**

When we have finished, we say:

**Blessed be the Lord,
of whose bounty we have received
and by whose goodness we live.**

Daytime Prayers

Many times during the day, we pray very short prayers.

Come, Lord Jesus!

Thanks be to God!

May the Lord bless us and keep us.

Our help is in the name of the Lord,
who made heaven and earth.

At noon, we ask Mary to pray for us.

Hail Mary, full of grace,
the Lord is with you!
Blessed are you among women,
and blessed is the fruit of your womb, Jesus.
Holy Mary, Mother of God,
pray for us sinners,
now and at the hour of our death.
Amen.

Dinner Prayers

We can sing one of these blessings to a familiar tune,
a tune like "Praise God from whom all blessings flow."

Be present at our table, Lord.
Be here and everywhere adored.
Thy creatures bless and grant that we
may feast in Paradise with thee.

We thank thee, Lord, for this our food.
For life and health and every good.
By thine own hand may we be fed:
Give us each day our daily bread.

Or this blessing:

All the world hopes in you, O Lord,
that you will give us food in our hunger.
You open wide your hand
and we are filled with good things.

Evening Prayer

Christians have long sung Mary's song (see Luke, chapter one) as their evening prayer.

My soul proclaims the Lord my God.
My spirit sings God's praise,
Who looks on me, and lifts me up,
That gladness fills my days.

All nations now will share my joy;
For gifts God has outpoured.
This lowly one has been made great.
I magnify the Lord.

For those who fear the Holy One,
God's mercy will not die.
Whose strong right arm puts down the proud,
And lifts the lowly high.

God fills the hungry with good things,
And sends the rich away;
The promise made to Abraham
Is filled to endless day.